CONFIDENCE PEARLS

KEEP THEM. OWN THEM. WEAR THEM.

MOFOLUWASO ILEVBARE

Confidence & Peak Performance Coach

CONFIDENCE PEARLS - KEEP THEM. OWN THEM. WEAR THEM.

DISCLAIMER

The author of this book does not dispense medical advice or prescribe the use of any technique, as a form of treatment for physical, emotional, or medical problems without the advice of a physician, either directly or indirectly. The intent of the author is only to offer information of a general nature to help you in your quest for a more productive lifestyle. In the event you use any of the information in this book for yourself, which is your constitutional right, the author and the publisher assume no responsibility for your actions.

All Scripture quotations are taken from the © 2016 King James Bible OnlineTM.

ISBN-13: 978-1543068153

ISBN-10: 1543068154

AQUA PUB

I dedicate this book to every person one who picks it up to read. You've come a long way, baby! The Confidence Pearls are my gift to you. Keep them. Wear them. Own them.

CONTENTS

"When I stand before God at the end of my life, I would hope that I would not have a single bit of talent left and could say, I used everything you gave me."

- Erma Bombec

spread
your
wings
and *fly*

ix

"Tell life's story through your eyes. Take us on a journey beyond the skies. Leap over the obstacles. Climb every mountain. Let your true self shine just because you deserve to be here."

- Mofoluwaso Ilevbare

x

Dare **to be**
different

mofoluwasoilevbare.com

"Pick up your brush. Paint! Colour Your World. Stop Hiding. There's no need to fear. God's got your back!"

Throwback Moment:
THE DINNER PARTY

Everyone was present at the farewell dinner. We had organized it to celebrate one of the senior managers, Derek, who had worked for three years on a special project and was now leaving. The catering service was great and the master of ceremony for the night was hilarious. He cracked jokes about good times and bad times and we had a good laugh. Three hours later, each person stood up to give their last hugs and I watched Derek whisper something in each person's ear. He must have whispered great words because I saw the faces lit up after every hug. Most of my colleagues were male and had gone before me—it was a usual occurrence to be either the only woman in the room or one of the very few. I waited my turn and walked confidently forward to give my farewell hug. I itched to hear his last words as well—after all, we had built a great friendship working together on this project. He beamed with smiles as he saw me approaching—his arms open wide ready to receive me. As we hugged each other, he leaned over and whispered in my ear "It was wonderful working with you these past three years but truly you work too hard. You should leave the playing field to the boys and spend your time at home to have kids and take care of your husband". I froze as I heard those words whispered into my ears. Whaaaaaaaat! Is that what you've been thinking all this time? I paused for a while, regained my stamina, then leaned towards him. "Thanks for your advice," I whispered back. "I'm very surprised you think this way. I've simply followed my passion every day being encouraged every morning by my husband to give my best. I wish you all the best in the future," I replied and walked hastily away.

Five years later, I am at a global project management meeting. As I walk in I glance around the conference room and the statistics reflect what I've been used to for many years. Yet again, I'm one of the very few women in the room.

WHY DID I WRITE CONFIDENCE PEARLS?

First, I am a woman and very proud to be one. Every day I see women struggling. Not only do they struggle to define their identity, to be heard, to find their purpose, to rise and be on top against all odds, but also to undertake education, to start a business, to master technology or to venture into areas that were once classified as 'No Go Areas', dominated by men. In the midst of political uncertainty and inadequate supply of basic needs, I see progressive men and women fighting the status quo and making a change, joining the UN launched #heforshe campaign in many parts of the world to support, promote and empower more girls and women. They achieve this collectively, through reformation in education, policies, grants, NGOs and public and private partnerships.

MORE HANDS ARE ON DECK. THERE'S STILL SO MUCH TO DO.

The United Nations sustainability goals and the various campaigns for gender parity are breaking grounds. However we still need to continue to raise awareness and educate a lot of men and women, both young and old, about the campaign for gender parity. We must serve as an inspiration to build rather than destroy, to strengthen rather than weaken, to support rather than envy.

My passion to see more women RISE, FLY and

SHINE motivated me to write this book. Each one of us must support, mentor and empower one another. Our future, based on equality, fairness, balanced societies, diverse leadership and empowerment depend on it.

WHAT I HOPE YOU WILL GET FROM READING THIS BOOK:

- An inner eruption to find and live on purpose every day.

- Simple steps to make the SHIFT you've been longing for.

- Inspiring stories to make you pick up your pen and write yours.

- Above all, a yearning to move from just a life of success to a life of significance, so that you truly become UNSTOPPABLE at work and life

I AM NOT ALONE

I am not alone

There are many like me

Brave and Outspoken,

We cannot be silenced

We are in, but not of this world

We cannot be bought

We cannot be silenced

I am not alone

My beauty transcends this bodily casing I wear

I refuse to give up, I choose not to fear

I've got too much value to share

I conquer my fears and fly.

Chapter One
BORN FOR THIS

"Whether you come from a council estate or a country estate, your success will be determined by your own confidence and fortitude."

~ *Michelle Obama*

There once was a little girl. She had lost her parents at a very young age and the only family she knew was her uncle who took her in and raised her as his own. As if losing her parents wasn't enough, one day, unexpectedly, a group of soldiers bombarded the house where they lived in. They took her away from the only place she called home and she ended up in the king's palace as a potential bride for the king. She found herself in an unfamiliar terrain with no uncle. That little girl was called Esther. Not having any other option, she settled in quickly to her new environment, followed every instruction she was given and applied all the beauty treatments religiously. On the night she was selected to appear before the King, she wore what was prescribed for her to wear. That same night, her status changed from that of a little girl from a lowly background. She became Queen Esther forever to be remembered as the Queen who risked being killed in order to save her whole nation from destruction. In her own words she said "I will go to the king and if I perish, I perish."

Confidence—the belief that you are terrific, a force to be reckoned with. It is the guts to move from just having a life of success to one of significance. It is the volcanic rush that erupts from your inside to achieve what others see as impossible.

Few know this, and Mosunmola 'Mo' Abudu is one the few. Mosunmola 'Mo' Adubu is a successful Nigerian media entrepreneur and talk show host. She is the founder of EbonyLife TV. She is using her media platform to change the way the world views African TV. Mo Abudu grew up in Kent, England, and in school she promptly became educated in racism. "I went to school in London and Tunbridge Wells. I was probably the second or third black person in that school and you find that you are being continually asked questions that just boggle your mind. Do you guys live in trees? Do you guys dance around fires? What do you eat for breakfast? Forever and ever, I always felt that I had to fight to prove who I was...."[1]

Abudu took this experience not as a hardship but as an opportunity. "Somewhere deeply buried in my subconscious was a need to tell Africa's story. My burning desire is just to tell everybody: "Listen, we're not a bunch of savages. We really are gifted." And she did.

In 2006, Mo Abudu decided to follow her dream of demonstrating the greatness of Africa through the eyes of the media. Her vision gave birth to Moments with Mo, the first syndicated African daily talk show, which later gave birth to the launch of her very own television station, EbonyLife TV, which today is truly at the pinnacle of African-inspired media and entertainment. You may never know how your life will turn out but you may also never find out if you do not try.

Don't ever put yourself at the bottom of the pile just because someone might snub you, reject your opinion, or diminish your truth. If you want to live a significant life, you must come to terms with the fact that not everyone will be on your cheer leading team.

Michelle Bachelet

She is not only the first female president of Chile but also the founding executive director of the United Nations Entity for Gender Equality and the Empowerment of Women (UN Women). Her devotion to reforming education in her country and protecting women's rights globally has not gone unnoticed. She was re-elected into office by her people.[2]

"Everything that happens to you is a reflection of what you believe about yourself. We cannot outperform our level of self-esteem. We cannot draw to ourselves more than we think we are worth."

~Iyanla Vanzant

Chapter Two

YOU'VE COME A LONG WAY, BABY!

"If we're afraid to stand in our own skin with those we work with,

then how do we lead those who have no voice at all?"

~*Ertharin Cousin*

Women Empowerment has come a long way. Today, many more leaders, organizations and nations are embracing the call for gender parity, education of girls, no child brides, and equal pay rights. Women Empowerment is not about making women strong. Women already demonstrate their strength through the hardships and struggles of everyday life. It's not about making women powerful. A powerful inner strength already exists in every woman. Women Empowerment is about EVERYONE joining hands to tear down the walls of segregation, stigmas, and unconscious bias in our societies; about enabling women everywhere to live to their fullest potential and contribute maximally in every sector they desire to contribute to. That way, the societies in which we live can truly develop and the future children of the world can call us blessed.

WHAT ARE SOME BARRIERS INHIBITING WOMEN FROM PURSUING THEIR DREAMS?

Cultural Expectations. Right from the primitive era, women always had the role of staying at home, bearing children and taking care of the family, including aged parents and extended members of the family. Women were expected to follow not lead, to remain silent not speak up, and cannot own land nor run a business. This meant many girls and women were not exposed to the outside world at all. Cultural traditions like this still hold strongly today in many parts of the world but some progress is being made too. Campaigns and more awareness is helping to take down some of these barriers giving women the same opportunities as men to obtain formal education, to work or even own businesses. More "working fathers" are sharing the load and the statistics of "stay at home" dads is also increasing. Nonetheless, the general perception is still that the woman should dedicate more time to her children and family regardless of her profession or level of education.

Less Confidence. In 2012, even though more than 126 million female entrepreneurs were either starting or running new businesses, in all of the 69 countries considered in the Global Entrepreneurship Monitor (GEM) 2012 Women's Report, women were on average still less confident than men in entrepreneurial capabilities in every economy field studied. In developed regions of Asia women showed the lowest levels of confidence in their abilities. For example, only 5 percent of women surveyed in Japan believed they had the skills necessary to start their own business. Yet this finding was not uniform: according to the GEM report, women in sub-Saharan Africa showed much greater confidence in their entrepreneurial capabilities. Four out of five women in Zambia, Malawi, Ghana, Uganda and Nigeria expressed confidence in having the skills necessary to start their own business and were less afraid to leave their comfort zone. Part of these higher levels of confidence in sub-Saharan Africa is owed to the fact that almost 60 percent of women know other women entrepreneurs and this gives them direct interaction with a role model.[3]

MOJISOLA SONOIKI

By following your bliss, you might discover the opportunity to do something you love and that makes you a living at the same time. Such was the case for Mojisola Sonoiki. A cultural activist, Sonoiki is the founder of Iyàlódè Productions, a company that creates programming for and consulting on film festivals and cultural events around the world. Mojisola recently completed a stint at IMAGE Film & Video where she was the first black woman to head the 18th Annual Out on Film Festival. She programmed the first African-American series ever shown in the Out on Film Festival.

In 1999, she created a film festival focusing on the stories and achievements of Women of Color. The first festival was called "E Wa Wo (come & see)—Sistahs in Film" showcasing films by Black women filmmakers from around the world. Shown in London, the festival sold out and received critical acclaim. After moving to Atlanta, Georgia, Mojisola started in 2005 the extremely successful Atlanta Women of Color festival in Atlanta which has now become an annual event.[4]

Fear of Failure. What if I fail? What if people think I'm a fraud? What if I make a fool of myself? A world of what ifs. Did you know that fear of failure is the #1 reason why many people do not try at all? The fear of failing can keep us so trapped that we never even step out of the closet. The fear of failure is also known as **"atychiphobia."** We all experience fear from time to time. It could show up through anxiety, venturing into the unknown and wanting to make sense of it all. The mindset shift is not to allow the fear to hold us back from living life to the fullest and achieving great things. To overcome fear is to embrace it like a gift- a gift that you choose to receive and then spin it around into some positive action. Everyone feels fear at some point. It's what we do with the fear that makes the courageous stand out.

Lack of Sufficient Role Models. In one of the local companies I worked for many years ago, we noticed that ladies were leaving after having been with the company just a little over a year. When asked why, the common statement each of these ladies gave independently was the following "I look ahead and there is no senior woman to inspire me. I am not sure this is a company where women can grow".

Everyone needs a role model. Everyone needs a trusted individual or individuals whom one can look up to, who can share experiences that can guide you into success in a faster and better way and who can keep you from making the same mistakes they made themselves in the past, a confidante who truly believes in you. This is what Joan Njoroge, Engen Mauritius MD revealed: "Like many young girls my dream was to be an air-hostess so that I could travel the world! It had never occurred to me that I could become the managing director of a company, working in a variety of countries. My aspirations were limited to the examples that were available to me at the time. Growing up I didn't know of women in senior executive roles. I therefore didn't aspire to such a position as I didn't realize that it was even a possibility," she explained.[5]

Let me tell you my story too. Growing up, I developed an overwhelming love for mathematics and physics. I dreamt of becoming an electrical engineer and as my university days drew nearer, I looked forward to studying as one. Did I end up studying electrical engineering? No, I didn't. I was talked out of it as it was deemed as "unfit' and "unlady-like". Looking around me, no woman in my family had studied electrical engineering, which also contributed to the feeling that my choice was inappropriate. Imagine if my family had a trail of awesome female electrical engineers, it would have been a no-brainer, right? That's the power of having role models or examples to look up to.

Who's your role model? Who inspires you to pursue your dreams? Do you have one? If you have at least one, that's great! In case you haven't found one, don't give up on your dream. Look around you more attentively. I can assure you there are many to choose from. Back then, there was no internet, but today the world is a global village and it's easier to find someone somewhere in the world around you who fits the profile you are aspiring for. Remember, it doesn't have to be someone related to you in any way. It may just be someone you admire, someone with similar values, or someone whose story resonates with you or challenges you. If you still can't think of anyone, rest assured you will have plenty of motivation to reflect and research by the time you finish reading this book. My encouragement to you is not only to find a role model, but also to lead the way and become a role model for many others. A confident woman is not afraid to lead where others dare not go.

"For the Lord will be your confidence, And will keep your foot from being caught."—Prov. 3:26

Lack of Capital: I asked a group of women entrepreneurs in one of my mastermind groups and they came up with this answer: the lack of awareness as to how to get venture capital or lack of availability of capital to drive ideas to execution. Supporting the family or starting a small business require resources which many women do not have. Luckily, this is all changing, thanks to the work driven by the UN, Women For Africa International, the Nelson Mandela Foundation, Melissa & Bill Gates Foundation, The Tony Elumelu Foundation, She Leads Africa, Cherie Blair Women Foundation, Women Economic Forum, many national economic forums, NGOs and partnerships with many international organizations, multinationals and academic institutions too numerous to count.

Limiting Beliefs. When a girl grows up hearing "A girl shouldn't be too ambitious", or "You are a girl, your place is in caring and taking care of your family", most often than not she develops into a woman who is afraid to pursue her dreams—a woman caged in her own body frame, abandoned to a world she is forced to believe she has no say in. This leads to diminishing self esteem, rejection, even self-blame and gradually that little four year old girl who was happy and excited about the world around her begins to crawl inside and play small and become less visible.

LUPITA NYONG'O

Lupita Nyong'o is a Kenyan actress and filmmaker. The Yale University graduate started her acting career in the late 1990s and as it is for most African women, the journey was bumpy for all sorts of reasons. According to Gundan (2013), it was not until 2013 that she had her major breakthrough following her award winning role as Patsey in Steve McQueen's film 12 Years a Slave. She actually won an Oscar for the best supporting role. While receiving the award, she made the remark that one's dreams are valid no matter where he or she comes from. This was a clear reflection of her own career journey, which started with a mere dream.[6]

Possessive Men. This could be a father or fatherly figure, a brother, a husband, a boss, or next of kin who see women as mere possessions and will not allow their women to work, to express themselves or travel to places. The belief that women are not equal to men is a limiting belief and can show up in men who will not support their women to build business skills, to own and run a business, or to pursue their "non-stereotype" dreams of becoming something great in life and in service to others. Sometimes the domination shows up through intimidation, oppression, through verbal and sexual abuse making the woman feel small, insignificant and irrelevant.

The Comparison Trap. A very common phenomenon is falling into the comparison trap—the self sabotaging trap that tends to push you into a demoralising state where you feel you're never enough. One minute you're feeling great your hair is growing but then you spot your friend's lustrous hair on her Facebook profile and it saddens your heart. One minute you're loving your curves, the next minute you're biting your nails wishing you had a psychedelic body like your new colleague at work.

Lack of clarity of vision. I asked the women in one of my Facebook groups what they thought inhibit women from achieving their dreams, and a vast majority mentioned this reason—they seem to suggest that many women don't even know what their dreams are, let alone how to pursue them. Can you identify with this issue? Do you know for sure what to do with your life to make it more meaningful and productive? Are you doing this every day? Vision brings clarity. Vision brings excitement. Vision opens doors to provision. Vision breaks barriers when things get tough. Granted, all the above might sound dismal, but the good news is that more women are finding their voice, seizing opportunities, and making a difference and that includes YOU. Maybe you identified yourself in one of the categories discussed above. Maybe you are still on your discovery journey trying to figure out who you are and what role you play in this world. I hope this book will create the momentum you need to take quantum leaps and ignite a "Yes, I Can" attitude in you. You've come a long way, baby!

Chapter Three
WHAT HIGHLY CONFIDENT WOMEN TOLD ME

"Whatever you envision, you can create. That life you desire, you can have. The very thing you are afraid of may be exactly what you have to do."

~Mofoluwaso Ilevbare

So, what do highly confident women have in common? Here are a few qualities I would like to highlight:

1. They Are Comfortable In Their Own Skin: Last year, I published the Confidence Journal for career women and in the introduction to the journal I wrote these words:

"A confident woman does not look for titles to validate herself, nor does she have to hide behind makeup. Instead, she starts from within. It is easy to talk yourself out of a bold step, saying that it is complicated and that life is unfair. I've been there and still catch myself doing that sometimes. But I have also learned that when you commit to your purpose, you not only live happier but also inspire many others to do

the same."

A confident woman accepts and loves herself for who she is. She does not need to look perfect in public and later hate herself when the lights are out and there are no fans around. To every woman of colour, your skin colour is pigmentation and nothing else. It is creativity at its best, thanks to God. If you want to dismantle stereotypical bias, IT'S NOT ABOUT BEING COLOUR BLIND. Colour is good! Acknowledge it. Appreciate it. Value it and SHINE through it.

"I am not tragically colored. There is no great sorrow dammed up in my soul, nor lurking behind my eyes.[. . .] Even in the helter-skelter skirmish that is my life, I have seen that the world is to the strong regardless of a little pigmentation more or less. No, I do not weep at the world—I am too busy sharpening my oyster knife."

—*Zora Neale Hurston*

2. They Appreciate the Good in Their Heritage: Growing up, I remember a rap song I loved so much with a chorus that went "I'm an African and I'm proud." Culture, they say, is a way of life driven by values we hold dear. We all grew up in a particular culture that shaped our beliefs, mindset and our socialization. By way of repetition, we have consciously and unconsciously developed certain concepts and behaviours which may be perceived by other cultures as either good or bad. Gaining a thorough understanding of your historical and cultural background can help you assimilate your feelings about your roots and turn them into a positive self-identity.

Gaining knowledge about yourself and your heritage can allow you to see all the more why you have to be self-confident and proud of whom you are. Until you learn more about yourself and embrace this knowledge in spite of it all, you cannot develop a great deal of self-esteem and confidence.

"A (wo)man cannot be comfortable without (her) own approval"

~ Mark Twain

Admit that there are things you cannot change about your past. For example, maybe your mother died at an early age, or maybe you never got to know your father. Maybe you are an only child, or maybe your parents couldn't afford your education. Maybe you were sexually abused as a little girl, or maybe you're currently experiencing difficulties related to your past; if you take a closer look, irrespective of all these, there is still something you can be grateful and thankful for.

QUEEN ELIZABETH II

Queen Elizabeth II, Britain's longest reigning monarch, also happens to share the same birthday as my husband. Her smile and poise when seen in public makes her lovable even by non-British people.

You cannot change anything about where you were born, why your accent sounds the way it does, nor the colour of your eyes (except with contact lens these days)— you have to learn to embrace the things you cannot change. Accept them and do not let them rule your life. Read books and listen to inspirational speakers that speak about your culture. This is one of the reasons I decided to write this book. Talk to the elders in your family and community who share your background, in order to glean their perspective about your culture. Learn from the positives. 'Don't throw the baby out with the bathwater.' Many things may still be wrong but many positive community values are also gradually fading away.

Become aware of the remarkable inherent strengths of the community in which you are in. Look at the strong values such as emphasizing togetherness and community, the focus on getting an education and improving oneself, the bonding of the family in times of need, and the strong sense of religion. Know your past. Consider doing an ancestry check. Though some may say "let sleeping dogs lie," who knows what you may find. Henry Louis Gates Jr. revealed evidence to Canadian-American singer and actress Gloria Reuben that her first great-grandmother connected her family line back to Africa. It changed her life.

3. They Have the Right Attitude About Everything: We live in an unpredictable world. The plans you made on Monday morning may get thrown out of the bus on

Tuesday because of a sudden airport strike, a currency market crash, or a call from your family doctor about a test result. An optimistic view of life can help you to keep worries away and to push you in the direction of your dreams. Embrace life more joyfully, with hope, optimism and good cheer. Enjoy better health, have happier relationships and experience greater productivity in your career; in return you can live a longer, more satisfying and successful life. Having the right attitude no matter what, is a key to your success.

4. They know Godfidence precedes Confidence: The truly happy and successful women are not ashamed to acknowledge the SOURCE of all wisdom, success and strength. It is not about you and what you can accomplish by yourself. In fact, the moment you stop struggling and surrender to God's leading and direction for your life, you'll realise things happen with much more ease—doors of opportunities will open and what could take others years to accomplish you will make it in record time. Putting your trust in God means that you understand you are limited and depend on Him for everything. He will never let you down.

5. They embrace their purpose: Not every woman is cut out to get married or have children and be able to combine that with owning a business or a leadership position in an organization, so whatever path or season of life you have chosen or God allowed to happen, embrace it. Be grateful for the many blessings and joys you share and spend less time moaning about the rest. If you'd take a moment to recall, you'll find those many blessings all around you. Things we take for granted. Privileges we may never know we have until we see someone who has not. Highly confident women know their strengths and put them to good use in both personal and professional situations. Learn to focus on what you excel in rather than dwelling on your opportunity areas.

6. They don't avoid doing the scary thing: Confident women don't let fear dominate their lives. They know that the things they are afraid of doing are often the very same things that they need to do in order to become the person they ought to be. *"The greatest mistake we make is living in constant fear that we will make one."* —*John Maxwell.* Don't keep your life on hold for fear of failing. After all, failure is just an eye-opener to another dimension of life.

7. They have a bias for action: Confident women know that a good plan executed *today* is better than a great plan executed *someday*. They don't always wait for the "right time" or the "right circumstances" before stepping out because they know there is no perfect time to step out on our dreams. They take action here, now, today—because that's where progress begins. They don't find excuses. Confident women take ownership of their thoughts and actions. They don't excuse their short-comings with defenses like "I don't have the time" or "I'm just not good enough". They make the time to do things that are important to them. They don't keep blaming circumstances or people around them for their failures. Instead, they learn from them quickly and move on knowing fully well that success and failure are both part of life.

ARIANNA HUFFINGTON

Arianna Huffington, co-founder and editor in chief of The Huffington Post shares her experiences after recovering from exhaustion by promoting the campaign of "get more sleep". Yes, more sleep! One of the many areas that got shoved away in our quest for more success; we sometimes tend to forget that sleeping well enhances productivity, not the other way round. Isn't it true that we make an emotional connection with people who have experienced what we are going through or have a similar story to share? What good habits are you spreading through your personal stories?

8. They don't obsess over the opinions of others: Confident women don't get caught up in negative feedbacks. While they do care about the well-being of others and aim to make a positive impact in the world, they don't get caught up in negative views that they can't do anything about. Don't get me wrong. "In the multiple of counsel there is safety" but not everyone's opinion matters. Learn to discern what advice is beneficial to your life's journey and choose wisely. Ask for the help of the Holy Spirit and HE will guide you.

9. They don't let a lack of resources stop them. Confident women can make use of whatever resources they have, no matter how big or small. They put creativity to work in utilising every available resource and never agonise over insufficiency. They leverage their support systems to get back up every time they fall down. They recognise that failure is an unavoidable part of the growth process. It is usually common to say "I have nothing" but in all cases God never leaves you with nothing. The real issue is that we think what we have is insignificant and cannot change anything.

10. They don't make comparisons. Confident women know that they are not competing with any other person. There's no rivalry when you're running in your lane. The only person you compete with is no other than the person you were yesterday with a goal of becoming a better version of yourself. Confident women know that every person is living a story so unique that drawing comparisons would be absurd and an exercise in futility. There is a proverb that says *the sky is large enough for all kinds of birds to fly in* and this is very true. Resist the temptation of belittling the greatness

CLARE ELUKA

Clare Eluka is the creator and formulator of the luxury skincare brand Premae Skincare. Premae Skincare is the world's first all natural, allergen free beauty brand for women of colour. The business was born from Eluka's personal struggles with Candida Albicans, or yeast overgrowth that was the culprit behind her acne and eczema. She discovered that certain foods that she commonly ate, such as wheat and milk were aggravating the condition. This led her to become a vegan and follow a gluten free diet.

This diet change healed her internal systems, and led her to begin to analyze her skincare products. She began to realize that, though many skin care companies branded themselves as natural skin care brands, the ingredients listed in their products were not all natural. This discovery led her to produce her own pure natural products. Her message: feed your skin as you would feed your body.

Eluka was the winner of the Women 4 Africa 2012 Educator of the Year Award. [7]

that God has placed in you. Say out loud with me "I am enough!"

11. They continually develop themselves. Every tree

needs to go through some pruning so that it grows well and bears fruit. Confident women don't limit themselves to a single plan or a single toolbox. They understand that competence fuels confidence and vice versa. This means the more you learn the more equipped you are to face life in general. The more equipped you are, the more confident you get to try new things and take new risks. Confident women are humble enough to learn from their partners, their colleagues, subordinates, lean in groups and anyone they come across.

12. They take self-care seriously. Women were created to nurture. This could explain why it is very easy for a woman to take care of everybody else except herself. After all, that's how you show you really care and are devoted to family, right? Wrong! That was my mentality growing up. My mum was the first to wake up and the last to sleep. In between those moments I hardly saw her take a rest. She worked all day in the classroom taking care of her students, her teachers, and the entire school, then after work, she worried about her husband, her children, the food in the fridge, the grocery shopping, the homework assignments, getting our hair done etc. Every Saturday morning, she was up again very early making the breakfast we would carry along to the farm at 7a.m. Her to-do list was endless. Half of those times as teenagers we didn't appreciate it. Instead I remember a few times I felt she was sticking her nose too much in my business deep down refusing to acknowledge I knew it was because she cared so much. I'm so grateful that despite all her struggles, my mum is still alive today enjoying her retirement and making out time to be with her grandkids. Mum, in case you're reading this right now , I'd like to say "I LOVE YOU MUM".

Now, the flip side to it is that many women end up sacrificing too much, neglecting their own spiritual, emotional and physical wellness and end up dying prematurely or end up stressed, overloaded, ill, and burned-out . Today, through hindsight and more information, this trend need not continue. Both men and women can join hands. We can do better to improve our quality of life without jeopardising the love for our family or the business needs. A mother who cares about her family and wants to be there in the long haul must learn to nurture herself. You cannot give what you don't have and if you keep pouring out and not refilling, one day the barrel will be empty.

13. They know when to ask for help. It takes more than one tree to make a forest. It takes a village to raise a child. In the same way, you must come to realise that it takes more than one person to raise a family or to build a career. How well do you take advice? How often do you ask others for help? Highly confident women understand the power of relationships and the downside of saying YES to everything. If someone else can help you, why not let them? God wants you to live a stress free life so use all the resources He has given you and surrounded you with.

MELINDA GATES

Melinda Gates, the cochair of the Bill & Melinda Gates Foundation appeared as the #3 in the 2015 Forbes "The World's 100 Most Powerful Women" recognized for her consistent delivery pioneering and spear gating the world of philanthropy and global development. A meaningful life is not so much about what you can get out of it but much more about what you can give back and influence others to do positively.

"If you want to unlock the most progress for the most people, start by investing in women and girls" —Melinda Gates

MY CHAINS ARE GONE

The bait was timely
Hooked me right on target
I pushed and turned
But there was nowhere to go

Then a big wave blew in
and dragged me back into the sea
Up on the waves I swirled
Breathless, I dangled to and fro

Suddenly it all became calm
I felt something solid beneath me
I opened my eyes and saw the shore
I also realized the hook was gone

"I must survive" I told myself
As I struggled to breathe again
"I will survive" I told myself
I am not a slave anymore

Chapter Four

PURPOSE & BABY STEPS

"If you can't figure out your purpose, figure out your passion. For your

passion will lead you right into your purpose."

~ *Bishop T.D. Jakes*

Keeping, Owning, and Wearing, Confident Pearls starts with finding and walking in God's purpose for your life. God has a life map created especially for each one of us. Some understand it very early in life and leap forward to success. Many others discover it later in life. Maybe as you read this, you are very clear as to your purpose and already following your passion, or maybe you're still trying to figure it out. Whichever way, transformation only begins when you figure out your WHY.

Authentic confidence begins with acknowledging the source of all confidence, God. It's like trying to operate equipment without reading the manual supplied by the manufacturer. You may find yourself wasting years trying to figure it out and in the process may render the equipment useless. All you have to do is read the manual or learn from the manufacturer and then you can instantly crack the code.

I'm usually fascinated by butterflies. I love the feeling of being free to fly and I haven't come across a butterfly that tries to crawl back into the cocoon after it's broken free. Even though its new environment may feel strange and unfamiliar, the butterfly flutters its wings a couple of times and then makes an attempt to fly. As it gains more confidence, it gradually spreads out its wings until it finds enough strength and momentum to soar high. It most likely never looks back after that.

"Self-esteem means knowing you are the dream."
~ Oprah Winfrey

Every woman's dreams and aspirations are just like those butterflies—trapped in human-made cocoons, breeding and growing, but unable to fly. Many things can keep our dreams repressed but the most powerful limiting beliefs are the ones we inflict upon ourselves.

"I am not good enough." This is the most common. The belief that you are not good enough because you are comparing yourself with someone or something else that you perceive to be better—your physical appearance, your social status, your level of education etc. If physical appearance had anything to do with who or what we can become, Ghandi may never have qualified as a leader. If riches had anything to do with it, Mother Teresa would never have stepped out and taken a stand on love, compassion, and peace.

To walk in your purpose and make a difference in life, you've got to overcome your fear of not feeling good enough and break out of the cocoon. So many people are stuck in the bedroom of life, suffering from the phobia of stepping out and being themselves, saying what they want to say, living how they should live, going where they would love to go. Others are living under the belief that everybody else is better, smarter, more beautiful, blah blah blah! (I bet you someone is envying you without you knowing). Would you rather hide your true self to avoid being judged by others or would you like to live freely? Would you like to escape that bedroom full of fear and find your way to being yourself—happy, fulfilled and free?

I'll let you in on a little secret… People will always judge you. First impressions, lasting impressions, in-between perceptions, and last minute conclusions—accept it! Everyone is entitled to their opinion, and as long as we've got seven billion people on earth, there's got to be twice as many perceptions to go round.

Who says you have to be skinny, or square-faced, or extroverted to be somebody, or to have a good life, or even to make a difference in someone else's life? Well, maybe the images in movies and media paparazzi add to this misconception but we all know it is pure entertainment, right? To break out of the cocoon, two baby steps you can start with today are: begin to shut your ears to all those horrible judgmental words your inner mind keeps whispering every five minutes and stop comparing yourself to other people's standards.

"I have no voice." Each and every one of us has a voice, a unique story to tell, an experience to share, and you don't need to win a singing competition to convey your message. You can express your voice in different ways - through your actions, through your writing, through mentoring, through whatever gift God has deposited in you. Fuel your purpose with passion and , fuel your passion with action. Your voice is not tied to something physical. It transcends the limitations of our human body. It springs from our spirit-from the core of who we really are.

"I cannot make a difference." the more you convince yourself that you are good enough and that you do have a voice, the higher the probability that you will get frustrated with the status quo repeatedly. Have you ever been in a situation where it seems your "body" wants to literally burst out of your body and protest when something isn't going as you expected?

Dissatisfaction with the status quo triggers thoughts; thoughts that can propel you to action, to speak up when others will not, to stand up for the truth no matter what, to lead a revolution to set things right. That belief fuels the passion of an "I can do" attitude and elicits motivation even when there is no particular reason to smile.

As the saying goes, "it only takes a spark to set a fire going." You may think "but girls like Malala spoke up and see what happened to her!" My answer to you is, imagine what would have happened years from now if she had not spoken up and brought the issue of girls' education to the surface!

Do you want to see a change in your life, your community, your world? It starts with you. Stop waiting for the government to get it right. Quit blaming it on your past or even on the society. Muster the courage to get tired of hibernating in the cocoon of life and break free. Start from where you are. Use your voice and begin to break down those walls.

"Therefore do not cast away your confidence, which has great reward."
—Heb. 10:35

Do you feel that your skin colour, hair texture or racial background puts you into a box? You don't have to feel this way. It's OK to be who you are. You have the power to become whatever you wish or alternatively to stay just the way you are. It's up to you. Embrace your unique style and personality. Embrace who God has made you and you will become who you were meant to be. Take a moment, close this book right now, and say these words until you hear them loud and clear in your spirit:

"I am good enough, I have a voice, and I can make a difference!"

How did that feel?

Since my intent with this book is to get you to erupt from the inside out, here are some ideas to help you rebuild your confidence and drive to make a difference:

i. Practice Expressing Your Thoughts or Opinions: Every woman must learn to develop her own unique way of expressing herself. Do it verbally and do it with the written word. The same way a butterfly needs to break out of its cocoon to fly, if you want to live a life of significance, you have to break out of your limiting beliefs and negative emotions that are holding you back. Your desire to break free has to become stronger than the emotional weight holding you down.

ii. Practice Assertion: Don't be invisible. Don't put your head in the sand. Don't be quiet when you know you should speak up. You have a voice that wants to be heard. Do you sometimes find yourself developing cold feet or too scared to express yourself in public? Try rehearsing your words before you speak and practice using "I" statements. Indeed the *meek shall inherit the earth*, but there are times to also make a *joyful noise!* Lend your voice and join many others to make a positive impact.

"You may write me down in history with your bitter, twisted lines. You may trod me in the very dirt, but still, like dust, I'll rise. "

—*Maya Angelou*

iii. Explore Likes and Dislikes, Interests, Disinterests: Know what gets you to groove—your favourite food, hairstyle, movie, musician, book, poet, sport—and take full advantage of including them in your life. For example, in the workplace, if you hate high heels but all the other executives in your company wear them, don't feel the need to conform. Be true to yourself. You won't get fired for wearing earth shoes to work. You may even get some compliments for your independent way of thinking and for being more sensible. As a consumer, spending lots of money buying what is in vogue simply to impress others, only incurs in debt and dissatisfaction because in the long run you would not be able to keep up.

LIVE YOUR PURPOSE

"But indeed for this purpose I have raised you up, that I may show My power in you, and that My name may be declared in all the earth"
—Ex. 9:16

Are you clear on your life's purpose? Do you know why you've been created? Without purpose you drift along lost, forever taking wrong turns down bumpy roads, going nowhere and accomplishing little. Or maybe you have found your purpose. Maybe you've always known that you were destined for something bigger, better and greater than what you are manifesting in your current life. However, although you have a million and one great ideas, you don't know which one is the one you were destined for and so you spiral into a start and stop cycle.

Be inspired by Erica Nicole, creator of YFS Magazine. She informs us, *"Many would-be entrepreneurs contemplate whether entrepreneurship is the right path, personally and professionally. I knew early on (call it a gut feeling) that I would transition from corporate America, in my early twenties, and become 'Young, Fabulous and Self-Employed'…. I was inspired to create YFS Magazine because I wanted to serve people. I literally asked God, "What did you put me here to do?" Our work is a gift—to us and to those we are meant to serve. Life becomes epic when you think less about how your gift serves you and more about what it can do for the world."* 18

That was Nicole's purpose. What's yours? Take a moment to remind yourself of it right now. You can even pause and write it down in your journal. If you're not sure, don't panic. I'll share some ideas to get you started.

But before, let me just remind you why this is important. Once you know your purpose for being on this earth, your life will become a joyful adventure, you will be eager to greet each new dawn, eagerly pursuing your chosen path. Things will flow and gradually fall in place. You will feel alive, charged, joyful, engaged; you will do what you love to do and all you can to accomplish it. Pulsing with electrifying passion and energy, you will draw the people, opportunities and resources you need. Start now to take the journey. Below are some ways to help you find your purpose:

i. Ask the Author of Life: Yes, ask God to show you His purpose for your life. Nothing is more satisfying than being exactly where you are meant to be and doing exactly what you were called to do. Learn to Dream. Dream of doing something important. Dream of making a better world. Dream of making your mark. Dream of walking into the door of an office that says, "Ms….. CEO." We were born to dream gigantic, humongous dreams, just like God. Don't settle for less simply because of your background or social limitations. If you believe in your dreams and start to take action, you can make things happen.

ii. Explore Your Desires: what do you desire from your life? Perhaps you would like to create a new make-up line for the busy working mum, or design an app for helping shy women become more assertive (call me up if you've got an idea we can partner on!), or hold a powerful place at the stock market. Desire puts you in touch with your authentic self. Fuel up, the skies are no longer the limit. Don't shy away from the BIG questions like the following:

- If nothing held me back right now, what would I do with my life?

- What is my ideal life?

- If I died today, what would I regret not having tried?

- What sparks my creativity?

- What would I do for free?

Take a moment to journal and if any other specific question comes to your mind, reflect on it too.

iii. Explore What Would Make You Feel a Success: everyone wants to feel successful and influential. What would make you feel that way? Not sure? Make a list of five things that you are burning to have, in order of priority. You may wish a million dollars—most of us do! But having it may actually be low on your priority list. High on your list might be to own a company that produces an organic cotton mop as this will help save the earth, or it might be to build a school in three to four less privileged cities many miles from where you live, or maybe you want to be the first female president of your country; just like Madam Ellen Johnson Sirleaf, who is the 24th President of Liberia and Africa's first democratically elected female Head of State.

"All girls know that they can be anything now. That transformation is to me one of the most satisfying things."

~ *Ellen Johnson Sirleaf*

DRESS FOR SUCCESS

Once you've discovered your purpose in life, let the way you dress reflect who you are. No amount of vintage clothes and designer shoes can cover up low self-esteem. You can only fake it for so long but true confidence will always outlast and shine through. Pay attention to your clothing and dress like the child of the King, the heavenly King. He created you to have dominion so act like it. The great grand-daughter of the Queen of England cannot dress anyhow, act anyhow or talk anyhow. By virtue of her lineage, she is bound by certain rules. The same way if you carry God's Kingdom lineage in you, you have to look the part.

As you follow your dream, dressing the part becomes even more critical. Here is what panelist Rita Mitjans, chief diversity and corporate social responsibility officer at ADP, is reported as saying at a recent summit:

"Part of what I wear is because it projects a certain image. If you yourself are not confident in an idea, it is going to come through. First convince yourself that you can win. It starts with your mindset and will affect your tone, your presentation, your image." [19]

MILK YOUR STRENGTHS

One way to explore this aspect is to first ask yourself "What am I good at?" Possibly more than you realize. What might you be good at that you have not yet tapped into? Think of what comes naturally to you. Perhaps it's computers, or drawing, or math, or writing poems. What compliments have others given you lately? If you're still stuck, you can:

i. Make a list of all the things you do well

ii. Ask friends and family to tell you what they have observed you do well

iii. In some cases, be courageous to try out new things. You never know if they would spark an interest in you.

For Adenike Ogunlesi, the founder of Ruff 'n' Tumble children's clothing line in Nigeria, it was sewing. *"I used to make clothing for women. So I decided that I'd just make some pajamas for my kids."* From a tiny shop, staffed mainly by her and her mother, 'Nike' turned Ruff 'n' Tumble into an instantly recognizable brand of clothing in Nigeria and it all started because she capitalized on her strengths. [10]

Don't focus on what you can't do. Focus on what you're good at and put your focus into developing those skills. People are smart in different ways. You can be great in science but have two left feet. You may not know a hundred words of vocabulary but can sing as passionately as Angelique Kidjo. You can align your unique talents, expertise and knowledge with what you're really good at and really enjoy doing. Then see what type of product, program or service pops into your head.

After spending some time with Nelson Mandela, Oprah Winfrey birthed a new dream. A dream to educate and empower girls. In 2007, the Oprah Winfrey Leadership Academy for Girls opened in South Africa. When she introduced one of its graduates to an audience at Stanford, she also shared some of the advice that she gives to "her girls", "Your real work is to figure out where your power base is and to work on that alignment of your personality, your gifts you have to give, with the real reason why you are here," she said. "Align your personality with your purpose, and no one can touch you."

CREATE YOUR LIFE PURPOSE STATEMENT

What do you envision as your mission in life, the thing that would make you feel that your time on this earth could have made a difference? For Winnie Mandela it was to ensure that her husband's message was heard while he was incarcerated. For Michelle Obama, former US First Lady, it was to raise awareness around childhood obesity. For me, it is to raise confident and influential leaders, men and women, who will be unstoppable at work and in life, and be the best God would have them to be.

What are you born to do? Here are some ideas:

- Teach people ways to conserve energy to help save the planet

- Like Wangami Mathai, get everyone to plant at least one tree to save our forests

- Make a million dollars so you can help support your parents in their old age and also build an old people's home for other aged people in your community

- Invest as much money as you can in your children's education so they can have a better life than you did

- Teach rural women how to be successful financially and enrich their families and communities

- Sponsor underprivileged children to learn to read so they can have a better life

- Become a successful entrepreneur and make enough money to help bring technology into agriculture in developing countries

When you can picture your purpose, you then have a clear direction. You know what degree you wish to pursue. You know where on the planet is the best place for you to live. You know what career path to pursue. You know what kinds of books to read and movies to watch. You know what to focus on and can sift through everything else happening around you.

Take a break right now , pause, reflect and note down your answers to the following questions:

i.   *Who are you as a person?*

ii.   *Why do you get out of bed every day?*

iii. What do you want the rest of your life to be about?

BE YOUR AUTHENTIC SELF

"If I didn't define myself for myself, I would be crunched into other people's fantasies for me and eaten alive."

~ *Audre Lorde*

Know thyself. It sounds easier than in reality, doesn't it? I know this because I've been through the same struggles too. From an early age, I was taught what girls should and shouldn't do. Puberty didn't help either. I was plump and short while the image of the perfect teen was to be slim and psychedelic. Getting into the corporate world, I have also experienced the impact of stereotyping and cultural bias of what an African woman can or cannot do. When you've had this kind of experiences, life teaches you that to get ahead you have to play the game in a particular way and please the powers-that-be. But despite all the gimmicks, you are still not free to be who you truly are. 'Image management' can be exhausting and emotionally depleting, especially if you are trying desperately to be liked, loved, or accepted. It only leads to discouragement and lower self-esteem.

It is time to stop struggling to be what you are not. You don't have to approach the world with a false persona. Being your authentic self is the key to your success both now and for the rest of your life. You must strive to live on your own terms and be true to yourself. You must learn to honour and express your authentic self. When you do, your true gifts will shine through at work and in life, and you will be valued for whom you truly are. The bottom line is: when something doesn't feel right, it isn't. In making a decision, follow your gut. Relish in the fact that you were created in the image and the likeness of God Himself. Why would you want to be like somebody else?

"One of the lessons that I grew up with was to always stay true to yourself and never let what somebody else says distract you from your goals. And so when I hear about negative and false attacks, I really don't invest any energy in them, because I know who I am."
~Michelle Obama

BE INSPIRED

"You are on the eve of a complete victory. You can't go wrong. The world is behind you."
~ Josephine Baker

Another way to find your passion and purpose is to find what inspires you. Perhaps it's reading about great heroes of the past. Take Madam C.J. Walker (1867–1919) for example: she was the first black woman millionaire in the US. Born as Sarah Breedlove, the daughter of former slaves, Walker went from being an uneducated farm labourer and laundress to one of the 20th century's most successful, self-made women entrepreneurs. Turning a problem into an opportunity, Walker took a scalp ailment that caused most of her hair to fall out and came up with some homemade remedies, founding her own business in 1905. Her first product was Madam Walker's Wonderful Hair Grower, a scalp conditioning and healing formula.13 Such excellence should inspire us all to follow our vision.

Who is your favourite hero/heroine? Perhaps it is the CEO of a company; perhaps it is your father. Try to immerse yourself in their lives and ask questions. Their positive energy may just rub off on you and, if not, at least you are learning from the experts how to get where you want to go. If you look in the Bible, there are many role models there, from Esther to Deborah, from Dorcas to Mary. The men are also not left out. Find a mentor.

Knowing what they did to make it to the top can help you get started or avoid mistakes. Of course their success didn't happen just because they were lucky. Great leaders and role models—each one of them had a dream and took steps to make it happen.

BETHLEHEM TILAHUN ALEMU

Bethlehem Tilahun Alemu's childhood village in Ethiopia taught her an eye-opening economic lesson: "We had lots of artisan talent, but no job opportunities," she says. So, on a plot of her grandmother's land in Addis Ababa, she created her own solution: soleRebels, a shoe company that pays fair wages and uses locally sourced materials such as organic, hand-spun cotton which cost less there. Now known as the "Fair-minded cobbler" Bethlehem informs us, "Most cotton farmers never use anything more than animal dung as fertilizer." And the soles are constructed from recycled tires. How successful has she been? The shoes have been featured in Urban Outfitters and Whole Foods. Today, Alemu has opened several stand-alone boutiques in Europe and also in the U.S. In the stores, customers are able to select their shoe model, colour, material (such as local Abyssinian leather), and trims; Ethiopian artisans will make the creation within two weeks. They will ship it worldwide, for free.[11]

KNOW YOUR VALUES

To be a confident woman leader, you must have a healthy self-esteem and this requires self-respect. Without it, you will remain insecure, striving to be someone you are not. To gain self-respect, you must make wise decisions that reflect your values and personal beliefs and remain true to your inner calling—your raison d'être, your WHY.

ASK QUESTIONS

"Now this is the confidence that we have in Him, that if we ask anything according to His will, He hears us."
—*1 Jhn. 5:14*

Leaders are curious. Confident women ask questions. They ask questions to fill the gaps between what they know and what they don't know. Some examples are: "What made you come to that conclusion?" "How do you know that's true?" "What prompted you to make that change?" "What other options can you try?" If you find yourself around children, observe them. One common thing you'll find with children is their high level of curiosity. The more questions they ask, the more their creativity widens and the more their knowledge increases. Sometimes it drives me crazy when I have to respond to every single 'Why" question my son asks. "Why do dogs wag their tails?" he asked me the other day. Questions raise awareness. Questions challenge status quo. It means having an inquisitive mind, which is not to accept things at face value but wanting to go deeper, and to have a critical perspective on things. Questions open doors to what is unknown. So, imagine if you never ask! You many never receive.

BE A LIFETIME STUDENT

Confident women are lifelong learners. They strive to grow, develop, improve, and evolve. Never has this been more important. Information travels at the speed of light in the 21st century, with knowledge changing by the sound bite. To be an influential leader, on-going learning must be an imperative! Take courses. Brainstorm. Ask around. Surf the net. Carry out some research. Learn, learn, learn! Fail and learn. Fall and get up. Read books. Great books change your life, books that you can't put down, that speak directly to YOU, that you absorb without effort. Try new things, like trying a sport, or going a day without eating meat, or taking Qi gong chi, or moving to another country, or befriending a person of a culture with which you are unfamiliar. The more new things you try, the more you will discover what fires you up and bring you closer to the discovery of your passion in life. Think of one new thing you can try every week.

FACE YOUR FEARS

"When I dare to be powerful—to use my strength in the service of my vision, then it becomes less and less important whether I am afraid."

~ Audre Lorde

Whenever you feel afraid, acknowledge it but don't let your fears cripple you. To grow, you must face and banish them. If you don't face and defeat your fears, those same fears may control your life and repress your ability to advance and become a confident woman. When I'm afraid, I say these words to myself over and over again: *"For God has not given us a spirit of fear but of power, love, and a sound mind" ~ 2 Tim 1:7 (KJV)*. How can you overcome your fears?

i. Pray: nothing beats a good old prayer of faith.

ii. Take the Bull by the Horns: "sink or swim." You've probably known someone who overcame their fear of water by being thrown into a lake, forced to paddle to shore. Look your fear in the face. Talk back to it. As Eleanor Roosevelt cleverly advised, "Do something that scares you every day."

iii. Write Down those Scary Desires: try writing down five things in your life you want but are afraid to go for. For instance, "I would love to visit Haiti and learn creole cooking, but I'm afraid to fly." "I would love to ask my boss if I could work some hours at home, but I'm afraid he'll fire me."

Write down next to each desire what action you could take to overcome your fear. For instance, "I am going to take a class to learn how to overcome my fear of flying. Then I'll be able to take that trip to Haiti." Facing your fears empowers you in the long run. Perhaps you want to start a business but you are too scared of venturing into the world of entrepreneurship. Here is what *Jessica Pruitt* suggests:

"You will go through a lot of personal and business development as you seek out new ways to keep the faith as you navigate the highs and lows of launching and building your business. Entrepreneurship will require that you push yourself past your limits and boundaries. There is no thinking outside the box, you have to throw the box away and constantly get outside your comfort zone."

iv. **Stand Tall:** when you are afraid, worried, depressed or sad, stand up straight. Why? When you feel defeated, you slouch and this posture actually makes you feel even worse. On the contrary, if you deliberately try to stand up tall, pulling your shoulders back, sticking your chest out and raising your chin, you will begin to feel a sense of confidence associated with power and authority.

STEP OUT OF YOUR COMFORT ZONE

The most crippling fear is the fear of failure. It emanates from an aversion to risk because you feel too vulnerable. Yet you must take risks to find your passion.

Success rarely comes without losses or failures. If you are miserable in your job, explore other possibilities. If one way doesn't work out, explore another. If a particular habit is holding you back from reaching your potential, make up your mind to do something about it or get some professional help. Have the courage to venture outside your comfort zone and explore new challenges. To grow and succeed in achieving our dreams, we must break through the safety net that we've built around ourselves. Every day, take one small step outside your comfort zone.

EMBRACE FAILURE

As failure forces you to take a different road, think of

it as a great opportunity, as your best friend. When things don't work out, rather than bemoaning what went wrong, figure out how you could have done things differently. The next time a similar situation arises, you will know better what to do; and if not, embrace each time you fail as a discovery of yet another thing that prevented you from succeeding. Each time you will be one step closer to your success. After sufficient incidences of failure, nothing will stand in your way.

"You may encounter many defeats, but you must not be defeated. In fact, it may be necessary to encounter the defeats, so you can know who you are, what you can rise from, how you can still come out of it."
~ *Maya Angelou*

DELAY GRATIFICATION

In the classic 'Marshmallow Experiment' of 1972, a

researcher placed a marshmallow in front of a young child with the promise of a second one if the child refrained from eating it up while he or she left the room for 15 minutes. Follow-up studies over the next forty years revealed that the children who resisted the temptation to eat the marshmallow grew up to have better social skills, higher test scores, a lower incidence of substance abuse, less obesity, and a greater ability to deal with stress.

Following your dreams and becoming a successful womanpreneur or woman leader takes time, persistence, patience, but also delayed gratification. You must wait for the big payoff. But delayed gratification could also mean foregoing your palatial dream house and becoming house poor in order to put money into a new business venture, or skipping the safari in Kenya to attend a convention in London to help you launch your new product, or even burning the midnight candle so you can get that degree.

GET FEEDBACK

I asked a friend of mine, a best-selling author, what is

the secret of her success. She told me, "I love when people red mark my manuscripts. It tells me what I need to work on to improve the writing." As you travel down your path to being a confident woman, expect feedback from others, lots of it. Welcome it. If it's negative, it will give you needed information about whether that was the right thing to do. If not, you can adjust and move forward. If you resist and become defensive to criticism, you are unlikely to achieve changes towards a greater growth. That could mean not just improving what you are working on but perhaps ultimately taking a different, better path. If you don't get feedback, ask for it. Without new information, you can't make the corrections needed to get you closer to your goal.

TAKE THE LEAD TO CHANGE

Good leaders are flexible. If the current method fails, then attempt something else or another method. Such flexibility makes you more adaptable to change, upping your chances of success. You also have an intuitive sense of when to respond and when to refrain. Confident leaders are also not afraid to change their mind and consider alternative points of view. Rather than focusing on being right, you should draw upon not only what you know but remain open to novel approaches to a problem, even if it questions your beliefs.

BE PERSISTENT

"When one door of happiness closes, another opens, but often we look so long at the closed door that we do not see the one that has been opened right in front of us"

~ Helen Keller

Leaders are persistent. They plough on right to the end until they get what they want, even if the odds are stacked against them and they fail over and over again. They have "grit." Grit means that you stick to a task until it is completed—no matter how long it takes. In other words, you mustn't give up easily.

ONYINYE EDEH

Her passion for girls' empowerment can be traced back to when she turned 13 years and was diagnosed with a hip condition known as Legg Calve Perthes disease, which has caused her to walk with a three-inch limp since her teenage years. She was not born with this condition, so dealing with her diagnosis as a teenager was not easy. Her friends often made fun of the special shoe she had to wear in middle and high school. One friend even named it a "pimp walk." Despite this challenges, Onyinye embraced her limp, was able to overcome self-doubt and esteem issues at a young age and today empowering others to love their bodies and know that nothing nor no one should ever make you feel like less of the person God created you to be. As the Founder and Executive Director of an international organization, Strong Enough Girls' Empowerment Initiative (SEGEI), Onyinye is nurturing a community of girls and women who know their worth and support each other's advancement and success. She was recently recognized by the Queen's Young Leaders Program for my efforts to empower girls. To support her cause, Onyinye can be reached via e-mail at: oedeh11@gmail.com

Having spent years studying kids and adults, psychologist Angela Duckworth was curious about what quality most predicted success. What did she find? Grit—all the way. Gritty people acquire higher-level degrees and college GPA (grade point average). They are the cadets who will tough out their first difficult grueling year at military school. Be careful though: grit is not perfectionism. Gritty people strive for excellence, by assuming an attitude that allows room for failure and vulnerability in the quest for improvement and, although there may be disappointments due to failure, they persist until they reach their goal.

But what if you're not gritty? What if you feel that you lack the innate abilities successful people have? Is there anything you can do about it? Absolutely! If you follow everything I have outlined in this book, you will begin to see yourself as a person who will persist and succeed at their goals—a person with grit.

PUT IN THE WORK

"....but the hand of the diligent makes rich" (Prov. 10:4b)

If you want to get ahead, you need to put in the work and persist, persist, persist. How many times have you had a great idea but have given it up after it failed, having tried it out only once? Success requires work.

In his 2007 best-selling book *Outliers*, Malcolm Gladwell calculated how much time you actually have to put into something to become a superstar. He did so by looking at the best of the best: the Beatles, Bill Gates, Steve Jobs and others who built empires of influence. It turns out it takes about 10,000 hours to become an expert in your endeavour of choice. It breaks down to at least 20 hours a week over 10 years. This is food for thought, isn't it? The message simply is that success does not come from mere wishful thinking, you need to act and work hard to achieve it.

EXPECT ROADBLOCKS

The road to success is strewn with hurdles, as you certainly know all too well. To become exceptional, you must not let all the criticism, ridicule, rejection and, maybe even racism, make you feel worthless. Be prepared and persist in smashing through these roadblocks. This is what a confident woman does. To give you the confidence to get past obstacles in your way, act as if you had already achieved your dreams.

START NOW

Act as if you only had a few months to live and no time to waste. Start your journey now—not tomorrow, not next week, but now!

Explore what you care about most and find your *why*. Explore what you are good at and create your life purpose statement. Above all, follow God's guidance and tap into

MS. KNIGHT K. MUTETI LANGAT

Knight is a young mother of one, married to Mr. Haron Langat. She holds a Bachelors Of Arts Degree in Social Work from the University Of Nairobi and currently pursuing a masters degree in Leadership and Governance at the Jomo Kenyatta University of Agriculture and Technology. Following the difficult challenges she underwent after the death of her father in 2012, that left her half-orphaned, she turned her loss into service to humanity. **Daughters of Kenya** was born in May 2016, a non-profit making charitable organization guided by Christian Values, Ethics and Principles working towards improving and changing the lives of the orphaned girls in Kenya with the belief that *every orphaned girl child should experience the love and security that only a family can provide.* Their main projects include a) Anti —Female Genital Mutilation in collaboration with the government Kenya Anti-FGM board, b) End Child Marriage in partnership with Girls Not Brides, c) household empowerment and mentorship for orphaned girls. To partner with her vision, visit *www.daughtersofkenya.org*

the gifts He embedded in you from the moment you were conceived. Believe you can change your life. Follow the good steps of successful leaders. Successful leaders question and solve problems, become educated, persist, plan and are intentional about their decisions. They think flexibly, keep an open mind, have patience and delay gratification. They face their fears, obtain feedback about their performance and then accept and adjust accordingly. They step out of their comfort zone and take risks. They accept failure and move on and they prepare ahead of time for obstacles.

AFTER THE STORM

Dark clouds of grey swept over the horizon
It was clear to me now, I was all alone
Friends had left me; each one had a perfect excuse

The voices in my head were my companions now
Badly wounded, my fingers caress my skin
Will this ever heal? Will I ever be whole again?

I know I have a purpose, a place to call my own
And what I feel right now may be tough
But not strong enough to beam it out of view

Help me believe I can get through this
Show me the path that I must go
Give me the strength to go through this
To believe that after the storm… comes a glow

Chapter Five

LIGHT UP YOUR WORDS

Do you believe you can become a highly successful woman framing her world and positively influencing the future? YOU MUST!

Words Create Reality

"Watch your thoughts, for they become words.

Watch your words, for they become actions.

Watch your actions, for they become habits.

Watch your habits, for they become character.

Watch your character, for it becomes your destiny."

~ Frank Outlaw

What are you thinking right now? Five minutes ago? Ten minutes ago? Inside your head is an on-going inner dialogue based on how you perceive your world and yourself. These thoughts, these words are incredibly powerful and create your reality. They become your self-image and unconsciously guide daily actions and decisions. They create the story of your life. Let me ask you another question. How do you want to be remembered? Like a fierce woman who impacted her world or one who merely passed through? Your choice. If you want to leave a great legacy behind, you will have to ensure that your inner dialogue is mostly positive: "I'm smart." "I'm beautiful." "I'm interesting." "I can make it." But this won't happen if your mind chatters mostly in negativity—"I'm fat, I'm stupid, I'm clumsy, I never finish anything; I can never succeed. I'm inferior." If these are the predominant thoughts that run through your life, you are unlikely to take the needed actions, unless you rewrite your self-defeating inner dialogue and replace it with a positive message. Only then will your self-esteem increase enough to give you the confidence needed to take the necessary action to get what you want out of life.

If you get stuck in the "poor me" mode, feeling a victim of your circumstances and blaming others for your problems, you will sabotage your goals of success. This victim mindset comes from feeling that outside forces control you—"Her intimidation made me nervous" or "The devil made me do it." You have what psychologists call an *external locus of control.* This means that you hand over to someone or something outside yourself the control of how you feel or what happens to you. As a result, you do nothing to change things because you feel too powerless to do so. Change this mindset to one with an *internal locus of control.* This will happen if you begin to feel in charge and in control of what happens to you. There's only one way to achieve this: you alone must take responsibility for what happens to you.

CHALLENGE YOUR BELIEFS

"Whether you think you can or you think you can't either way you are correct."

~ Henry Ford

What makes you feel like you are not in control of your destiny? It's probably because you feel that no matter what you do, you never seem to get what you want. Maybe you don't really believe that you have what it takes to change your life for the better. But this is a false, self-destructive belief. For instance, let's say that you feel that you will never be able to save enough money in this economy to start your own business. Is this absolutely and irrefutably true? Can this really never happen? Unlikely—this maybe a false belief. Here's another one. You find a closed door. Automatically in your mind, you believe the door is locked, but instead of attempting to open the door you turn back. Did it occur to you that maybe the door was probably just closed but not locked and all you had to do was to turn the knob and walk into your moment?

Here are some common examples of false beliefs that could be holding you back:

- I never win anything.

- No one will listen to me

- Things like this don't happen to people like me

- I will never get out of my current life situation

- I'm too old to get married

- I'm to old to start something new

- If I go in a different direction, others will think I'm foolish

- I'm unworthy of success

- What limiting thoughts have you had lately? Add to the list.

To light up your life and live the best life as God intends, you must change these irrational beliefs. How do you achieve this? By challenging your false beliefs and talk back, refute and reframe them. When you catch yourself having a negative, self-defeating thought, re-frame it to a positive one.

Here are some examples:

Negative statement: "I'll never be rich."

Change to: Money and riches are for me to enjoy. I always have more than enough.

Negative statement: "I hate my thick black hair or freckled blonde curls."

Change to: My type of hair can be challenging but with some effort it can also be very beautiful.

Negative statement: I will never have my own company.

Change to: With enough work, diligence, and walking in God's purpose, I have the ability to get what I want out of life.

Every time you think negatively, ask yourself, "How is this serving me?" If it doesn't, re-frame it and toss the initial thought into the mental trash can. The more you entertain a positive thought, the more powerful it becomes. For instance, let's say you are working hard at building up your art handbag business but you keep running into obstacles which hold you back. If, every time this happens, you mutter to yourself, "This too will pass. I will persevere and succeed" this positive thought will become your belief. If you put time, attention and energy into negative thoughts and, for instance, obsess over a loss of business because your supplier sent the bags late, the negative or unwanted thoughts will override the positive.

There are things that might not change overnight, but if you learn to repeatedly refute negative thinking, eventually it will slowly diminish and be replaced by more rational, balanced thinking. So, start now. Make a list of your positive traits. Take a moment and think about it. Many times, we focus so much on what we are *not* that we overlook what we *are*. These traits can be physical, academic, or work-related. For instance, you could make a list of the following attributes:

- I have beautiful, radiant skin.

- I am a hard worker.

- My legs are strong and healthy.

- I am intelligent.

- I am a wonderful friend.

- I am creative.

- My body is gorgeous.

- My memory is blessed.

Keep this list handy for when you are feeling down or not so great about yourself; hang it visibly in your bedroom, or on your refrigerator, or keep a small list in your wallet for easy access around the clock. When complimented, get in the habit of saying, "Thank you," rather than refuting the compliment. When life throws at you some unpleasant realities, ask yourself the following questions:

- How can I view this in a positive way?

- What does God's word say about this?

- What is to be learnt from this experience?

- What are the other things in my life I am grateful for right this moment?

"By faith we understand that the worlds were framed by the word of God, so that the things which are seen were not made of things which are visible."

—Heb. 11:3

MY SMILE, MY CHOICE

My smile is a choice

My smile is gold

Tough winds sweep across my face,

sometimes making me squint in pain

My smile is a choice

My smile is gold

I know God loves me

and He's working it out for my good

Chapter Six

SPIRIT-BODY-MIND PEARLS

To become a confident woman, you must have the energy, clear thinking, and calmness of mind and body to feel confident. I have not found a woman who has only one role—the average woman juggles at least two roles amongst the following: entrepreneur, wife, mother, sister, daughter, aunt, charity organizer, employee etc. We are constantly switching roles, for instance between taking care of family members and/or establishing a business. To be able to fulfill all these roles effectively without breaking down, you must live a healthy lifestyle—feeding body, mind and spirit. Daily stressors weigh us down. We eat garbage food (all in the name of speed and efficiency) and sometimes some of us are too busy surfing the net to even take time to move our bodies. This will not help you to reach your goals. You need to love your body, feed it well, learn to relax, and feed your spirit, the inner core of your being.

FEED YOUR SPIRIT

"Man is a spirit, he has a soul, and lives in a body" is a common phrase I grew to love while in the Victory Christian Fellowship (V.C.F.) at the university. Authentic confidence cannot be faked. It oozes out from the depth of your spirit. If your spirit is not well fed, nothing else makes any sense. The things that are unseen drive the things that are seen. Let's look at some of the ways to feed your spirit positively.

Study the Bible. Everything we need to succeed in life— the laws of leadership, proverbs, instructions for living, how to deal with clients and neighbours, how to handle people who hate you, ways of controlling your anger—can all be found in God's word. Practicing the wisdom and daily instructions from the Bible strengthens the spirit.

Leverage Spiritual Resources. Digesting spiritual resources in the form of praise, worship, book, prayers, fellowshipping with others, going for retreats, listening to inspiring sermons and testimonies, can all strengthen your heart, give you hope, keep you motivated and fill your heart with thanksgiving and joy.

Exercise Godly Gifts. We all have unique gifts, carefully gifted to us the moment we were conceived in the womb. Discovering your gifts, developing them and using them to bless the world around you, is a great thing to aspire to. Everyone has been endowed with a unique gift, and that includes you. Your gift makes you stand out above the rest, it gives you leverage and makes room for you with Kings in high places. What's your area of gifting? Are you leveraging it daily?

Grow. There are growth milestones which you expect babies to exhibit at different stages of development. If the baby is not showing any progress the parent gets worried and seeks professional help. In the same way, are you growing spiritually year after year? Is your capacity to love ever growing? Are you less irritated? Do you show more empathy for others? Do you give more? If people around you cannot see your life changing positively and you cannot say for sure that you are more connected with God; then you might have what is described as 'stunted growth'. As you mark your birthday every year, take a moment to reflect on what has changed in you with respect to the previous year: habits, temperament, capacity to love, praying more etc.

NURTURE YOUR BODY

"When I take care of myself, I am confirming my worth to myself. If I give to myself first (time, rest, love), I have more to give to others."

~Oprah

Let's face it—women are usually under the spotlight, sometimes feeling the pressure of the humongous media sentiments of what a woman's perfect body and lifestyle should be like. In the workplace you may be among the very few women in your field or sector. This can sometimes intimidate you or cause you to feel different. Is your hair or skin, accent, educational background, country of origin good enough to compete? Such rumination leads to a profound lack of confidence in oneself. How can you build confidence in your appearance? The first step towards having lasting confidence is learning to love the body you're in. When you know that your body looks the best it can look, you will carry yourself with pride and respect.

Love those Curves or No Curves. In case you haven't noticed, women have different body types and many are far from a size zero. Many women have curvy, voluptuous bodies and will never look like Naomi Campbell, especially if wearing only a bikini. Kambili Ofili-Okonkwo however was determined. She wanted to find a stylish swimsuit that covered some of the areas she wasn't comfortable showing off, but none seemed to exist in Nigeria. Her only option was to buy sexy bikinis from overseas. Fortunately, she had a background in materials science, engineering and supply chain management and started to create her own line of swimsuits—beach attire that was practical and appropriate for the body conscious woman. Soon, friends and family started requesting versions for themselves. She invested $25,000 to launch the indigenous African swimwear brand KAMOKINI, a rapidly developing enterprise, by focusing on Africa's emerging beach, pool party and resort market.

All bodies are uniquely different. Love the body you WEAR—whether it is skinny, curvy, or heavy—and you will feel good to reside in it.

Practice Good Hygiene: Looking and smelling your best will do much to boost confidence. Keep yourself well groomed.

• Use soaps and shower gels that help enhance your skin. There are many natural ingredients available today as well. Use deodorant, preferably natural (crystal deodorant sticks work fine), brush your teeth upon waking and before sleep, floss your teeth once a day, and wash your face with a deep cleanser in the am and pm.

• Find a fantastic scent that you love and make it your trademark. Lavish your body with natural oils, creams, and powders imbued with essential oils that will not only add scent but good emotions. Make your skin last long enough to fulfill your life's assignments.

• Have a Daily Beauty Routine: since adolescence, you've likely stood in front of the mirror for hours, practicing different types of beauty routines based on your natural skin and hair type. Learn what daily regimen you require to stay fresh and healthy.

Your Hair Rocks. One of the first things you notice when you look at a woman is her hair. It is a natural endowment and part of her beauty. Learn how to treat your unique hair type and the regimen you require to maintain healthy and luminous hair. Whether straight hair, grey hair, brown hair, or thin hair, love your hair type and take good care of it. If you've got kinky and curly hair, there are endless products now available to create beautiful locks. Embrace them! You can wear your hair curly, straight, loose, kinky, braided, or in whatever style your creative mind comes up with. If you're unsure how to create and care for your beautiful hair, check out the many online resources available or visit a professional hair salon around you. The most important thing, though, whether it's natural, braided, relaxed, or weaved is to keep it clean and healthy.

Hair is a big business for women generally. In recent times more modern options are being provided to African women—or of African descent—to the point that the black hair care market is now worth a whopping $500b; hence international investors are beginning to pay more attention. Hair extensions are an option many of us use too. Venture capital firm Andreessen Horowitz led the $10m 'Series A' for Mayvven, enabling hair stylists to sell extensions directly to their customers if they wish. In 2013 however, Ngozi Opara, former financial analyst and trained cosmetologist, realized that no options of hair extensions existed that were made specifically to match the hair texture of women of colour. She went to work and launched Heat Free Hair, the first manufacturer of virgin hair created exclusively to blend with textured, kinky, and curly hair. In no time, celebrity clients started wearing her hair extensions including: Orange is the New Black actress Uzo Aduba; reality TV star Tamar Braxton; and singer Jill Scott.

Perhaps you too can be the next retail international heavyweight in women's hair care.

Fortify Your Body Engines. To function at your best, you must nurture the temple in which you reside, the one which acts as your visible display to the world. Do you? Consuming food loaded with processed, refined, chemical-laden fat, salt and sugar can make your brain foggy, your mind depressed and sick, your body sluggish, and your goals to rise, fly and shine will be sabotaged.

To be healthy, energetic, clear minded, upbeat and excited about life you need to be conscious of the food that you put into your mouth. What food should you eat? Whole, plant-based food, or in other words the food our bodies were designed to eat, digest and assimilate. These types of food will fuel your body with all the vitamins and nutrients it needs for optimal functioning. Try to maintain a balanced diet of lean, grass fed meats, non-gluten grains, and plenty of organic fruits and veggies. Also you should drink eight glasses or more of water each day for radiant skin. (I still struggle with counting how many glasses I take every day. Just make sure you drink regularly).

Move Your Body. If you aspire to be in the corporate world, sloth will be an unwelcome effect as you spend your day glued to a chair, staring at a computer screen for hours. This is a horrific problem for modern people. Not moving is anti-biological and will result in possible obesity and loss of firm muscle tone.

Moving your body for all its worth is the best pill you can take to give you the energy, disposition and brain power you need to take control of your life. Vigorous movement releases good chemicals for thinking, focusing, learning, and memorizing (noradrenaline), and wiring up the brain to make more efficient connections. These neural connections enhance memory, mood and learning, reduce anxiety and depression, foster brain growth, and lead to better sleep. To keep your body toned and in good shape, exercise regularly, ideally to the point when you break a sweat. If you can't, even taking just a leisurely lunch stroll through the park every day, or grooving to your favourite music while preparing dinner will empower you.

Don't Skimp on Sleep. In this on-the-go, over-committed world in which most of us live, and especially those of us in the corporate world where many must try to cram a week into a single day, sleep often suffers. This is bad for us in every aspect of our functioning. Quality sleep plays a crucial role in immune functions, metabolism, memory, learning, and other vital functions, making it essential for physical, emotional, and mental health. While you're asleep, your internal organs work at rejuvenation while your brain is busy filing away the day's information. When you don't get enough sleep, you wake up crabby, tired and spacey, thinking irrationally and making poor decisions. Clearly this will never get you into leadership in the corporate world. To function at our best, most experts recommend that we get around seven to nine quality hours of sleep. Without enough rest, we are stumbling through the day on too little sleep, and our mental health and self-perception could be at risk.

Here are some ways to ensure we get a better sleep:

• Go to bed early and at the same time each night to set your body's natural circadian rhythm

• Avoid stimulating activities before bedtime, like watching action TV or working at the computer

• Dab a few drops of lavender essential oil on the bottom of your feet at bedtime

• Increase daily exercise

• Don't drink coffee before bedtime or eat chocolate as the caffeine content will keep you awake

• Listen to soothing relaxation tapes

• Invest in quality bedding and pillows that enhance good sleep.

NURTURE SELF: "Oh How I Love Me!"

"When you smile the whole world smiles with you," as

the lyrics of the song go. How true. Tons of studies show that smiling can make you feel more positive and happier about yourself and your life. And the best way to do this is to smile at yourself while standing in front of a mirror.

Each morning, before going out into the world, do this mirror technique. Stand in front of the mirror, posture straight, shoulders pulled back. Take in a deep breath and flash those pearly whites. Notice what you admire about yourself; perhaps it's those deep almond eyes, the dimples on one cheek, your radiant skin, or your trendy hairstyle. Relish your beauty. Smile. Smile. Smile.

Take Time to Unwind. Stress is likely to be a constant companion as you attempt to keep up with the relentless demands on your time and brain. There is a good chance you will also be responsible for taking care of the children, the pets if any, running the household or caring for the aged. This leaves you at great risk for burnout, and even illness if you don't take the time to unwind.

Under stress, the sympathetic nervous system fires and produces the "fight or flight" response. The body goes into high gear: the stress hormones cortisol and adrenaline are released; the heart rate speeds up; and blood gets shunted away from organs into muscles, causing the body to tense up. As we need to react immediately, thinking processes don't work well, and poor focus and clarity lead to poor judgement. To avoid getting caught in this trap, you have to include stress relievers in your daily to-do list. One of the best ways to de-stress is to get in the habit of taking a moment to stop and breathe—to be in the moment. This will help slow the world down so you can get off for a moment, before tomorrow, next week, next year has arrived and take pleasure in experiencing life as it is unfolding before your eyes.

Too often, many of us carry around hurts from our past—regrets, shame, anger and pain, etc.

"Holding onto anger is like drinking poison and expecting the other person to die."
—*Nelson Mandela*

The way to stop such negativities related to the past from robbing you of your happiness is to acknowledge them and then move on. Remember, you can't change what happened to you in the past but, with a change of attitude, you can change what is happening to you right now. Forgiving others can set you free from a life of regrets.

Be refreshed by nature. God has made a beautiful world. Look all around you. These days, smart phones keep us glued to the screens so much that we don't have time to raise our heads and look around us. The world is a natural wonder. Connect with nature's bounty. Go for a walk in the woods, mountains, down the street, or along the river or ocean shore. Notice how peaceful you feel. I always wake up to the sound of birds chirping from a tree close to my bedroom window. I'm sure if I could translate the melody, they would be screaming "What a beautiful day!"

Create a Blessing List. We are all so rushed and overloaded with responsibility that we often neglect doing things that we love. Vow today to do at least one thing every day that you really love but don't get to make enough time for.

Here are some ideas:

- Read the Bible.
- Call a family member.

- Listen to inspiring music.

- Stroll around your garden.

- Take inspiring photos.

- Enjoy a relaxing massage.

- Slither into a bathtub. Use essential oils, fragrant gels, candles, and soothing music.

- Watch movies and read books that lift your soul. If you're sad, watch something inspiring or spend time in worship.

- Create something—a painting, a song, a dance, a skit, a story

- Get a facial, a manicure, or a pedicure. Plan a special pampering day at the spa.

- Go somewhere that is special to you, your own sanctuary.

- Spend time with those you love.

- Volunteer and help the needy, the orphans, or the refugees.

Establish Healthy Connections: avoid toxic people. Your hair is a frizzy mess." "You're a clumsy oaf?" "You'll never get that job." Stay away from "energy drainers"— people who suck the life out of you. These are the people who are quick to criticize on the pretense of *helping* you, who give endless advice on how to live your life when their own life is a mess, who spread negativity with every word they utter. Think of these people as dark clouds. When they disappear, the world brightens. So make every effort to keep these negative people at a distance as much as possible.

"[...] love those with whom you sleep, share the happiness of those whom you call friend, engage those among you who are visionary and remove from your life those who offer you depression, despair and disrespect."

~Nikki Giovanni

"Your hair is a frizzy mess." "You're a clumsy oaf?" "You'll never get that job." Stay away from "energy drainers"—people who suck the life out of you. These are the people who are quick to criticize on the pretense of *helping* you, who give endless advice on how to live your life when their own life is a mess, who spread negativity with every word they utter. Think of these people as dark clouds. When they disappear, the world brightens. So make every effort to keep these negative people at a distance as much as possible.

Of course, you can't always do this if the energy drainer is a family member, co-worker or close neighbour; but you can minimize contact with anyone who makes you feel inadequate, inept and unlovable. And you can lead by example by being the solution you wish to see in the world.

Talk about positivity in the news, friends with good fortune, excitement about your latest project, whatever you can talk about that is positive, something the other person can relate to, even if all you can do is disarm their negativity, even if only briefly. Don't allow them to dump on you. You cannot change these people and will only feel frustrated, discouraged and drained in trying to do so. They are not just negative towards you; this is their modus operandi, a projection of their own reality—their personal attitude. Even when they criticize or insult you, it may have nothing to do with you and everything to do with projecting their own insecurities and misery onto you.

If you feel guilty and find it hard to pull back, especially with close relatives, tell yourself that your well-being is too important to have someone cloud it over. Also, pray for such people. Give them feedback when appropriate. Every time you remove negativity from your life, you open it up for more positivity. When a dark door shuts, a bright one is more likely to open.

Seek out like-minded people. Confident people attract others like them. The people you hang out with have an impact on what you become. If they are cynical and negative, you are in danger of becoming cynical and negative too. If they are upbeat, smart, driven and confident, you are more likely to feel the same. Judge every relationship—and every situation—as to whether it's life giving or life taking. Relationships should help you, not hurt you. Surround yourself with people who reflect the person you want to be. Make sure your friends are people you are proud of knowing, people you admire, who love and respect you; people who make your day a little brighter simply by being in it.

Ideally, try to surround yourself with positive and supportive people, who believe in you, encourage you, are like you and align with your beliefs, and values. Their positive energy will motivate, energize, and inspire you.

Furthermore, try to find mentors who understand the challenges you're facing and can inspire you to greatness.

FEED YOUR MIND

The mind, or soul as others call it, is the seat for our emotions. Remember, we all have a destiny that needs to be nourished and that includes having a higher purpose in life. Let's look at some of the ways to feed your mind positively.

Learn to Forgive: we all have experienced anger, cruelty and injustice—black women even more so than other women. And this may leave us with feelings of anger, resentment, and even desire for revenge. Don't let these feelings eat up your time and positive energy. Doing so will leave you stuck in the past and make it hard to get ahead. People make mistakes. Forgive those who have hurt you or you will not be free to move on.

Practice Gratitude: do you tend to focus more on what

you don't have than on what you do have? Many of us do. Focusing on that will only increase negativity and decrease your self-confidence. Have an attitude of gratitude; and if you like the idea, keep a daily gratitude journal. Learn to count your blessings rather than to focus on your unfulfilled desires. Before going to sleep or when you awake in the morning, get into the habit to write the former down. On some days you will have amazing things to write. On other days though you will just feel grateful for simple joys. This habit is a daily practice I encourage in my book, the Confidence Journal for Career Women.

For days when nothing extraordinary seems to happen in your life, here are some ideas of what you can be thankful for:

- being alive and knowing you are loved by a lovable God,
- your mate, children, another loved one, or your pets,
- living your purpose,
- going out and coming back home safely,
- employees who will go the extra mile for you,
- business that is going well,
- close friends,

- good health, and

- peace of mind

Pay It Forward: what goes around comes around as the saying goes. A spirit of generosity should come hand in hand with your success. At least some of your bounty should be used to help others, financially and with acts of kindness. Be willing to give cheerfully to others. Smile first. Compliment strangers. Open the door for a senior. Be your beautiful self. It's much harder for someone to be indifferent, demeaning or being hostile toward you in the presence of love and kindness. By "paying it forward," you will reap rewards in gratitude, in making someone happy and even in changing others' lives.

Chapter Seven
A LETTER TO YOURSELF

If you want to become an authentic and confident woman living a life of significance and making a difference in the world around you, what you do after reading this book is key to your success. It's not enough to have knowledge. Mere knowledge does not produce power. It is the way knowledge is applied that creates power to transform. So, it's time to transform any thoughts this book triggered in you into actions and the best way to do this is to create actionable goals.

Maybe by reading this book you have been able to identify one or two areas you want to step up—goal setting enables you to accomplish that. Be intentional in taking control of the direction of your life. Goals are a great benchmark to help you determine and measure your progress. You may want to start a business in recreating classic fairy tales for children with a black heroine, or starting a girls' leadership club for local schools around your area; but simply wanting it won't make it happen. You need well-defined steps to reach your goal. For instance, you need to know first how to get started. How much will it cost to hire the team you'd work with? How much start-up capital will you need? Where can you get sponsors? And so on.

WRITE IT DOWN

Having this book in your hand is a testament that I have achieved one of my goals for the year. I've never been strict about New Year Resolutions but I believe in the power of writing things down. They say "the shortest pencil will outlast the smartest brain" meaning that if you keep a written record it would outlive the writer. I wrote down my dream of writing 10 books this year, one for each speaking engagement or training workshop I am invited for and the one in your hand today is the first. Writing down your goals helps you crystallize the "what" and the "how".

DON'T JUST SET SMART GOALS

Many of us already have read or heard in seminars about setting S.M.A.R.T goals. where S.M.A.R.T. is an acronym for Specific, Measurable, Achievable, Realistic, and Time Based. Yes, setting S.MA.R.T. goals can indeed take you far but I'd like to expand your reasoning around this concept. To set up your game, having SMART goals may not be enough. In the ebook "Uplift Your Goals", I share eight new perspectives to consider. You can download a free copy at bit.ly/upliftyourgoals

Are your goals:

Challenging? To bring the greatest personal satisfaction, set goals that push you to "raise the bar". Challenging but realistic goals should force you out of your comfort zone but not so far that you land in quick sand.

Exciting? Set goals that fire you up. Remember, the most important thing you must do is to identify your "why", your reason for being on this earth. Then create goals to meet this desire.

Actionable Now? Set goals that you can start NOW. It's

wonderful that you may wish to become a classical pianist when you retire, but that may be far in the future. You need to get fired up and get going now!

Worthy? Set goals that will serve others, that "pay it forward." Your message, product, service, art and so forth must serve the greater good of others, for instance of other black women. Ideally, it should not harm the environment. That means that if you wish to start your own cosmetic line, don't use chemicals in the ingredients that could potentially harm both the environment and the consumer. All the millions in the world are worth nothing if they are ultimately part of the problem, rather than part of the solution. To truly impact the world, you must create something that will make the world a better place for generations to come.

Positive? Be assertive and write your goals in positive terms. Write "will" rather than "would like to" or "might." For example, "I will spend an hour online tomorrow marketing my spices" not "I would like to spend an hour tomorrow...." Say both statements out loud and you will immediately feel how much more motivating the first statement is.

Detailed? Write out detailed goals. If you wish to be a millionaire, state specifically how much you wish to make every month and what steps you will take to reach your goal.

Visible? Try to read your goals out loud when you wake up in the morning and before you go to sleep. Post your goals in visible places: walls, desk, computer monitor, bathroom mirror or refrigerator to remind yourself every day of what it is you intend to do.

PRIORITIZE

After you have made a list of your goals you should prioritize them. Remember to consider your season of life while you prioritize. If you have young children for instance, creating a company that will require regular international travel may not be in your or your family's best interests. If you don't set your goals by priority, you may feel less committed to them nor will you be highly motivated.

Set Short and Long-Term Goals. Divide your goals into short-term goals—for example creating local interest in your new line of African spices—and long-term goals, for example creating an international e-commerce site for your spices.

To help you get motivated, jot down five short and long term goals that you want to accomplish. Short-term goals should focus on what you can manage in the next thirty days. Long-term goals are about what you want to accomplish over the next five to ten years. Remember to write them out in specific detail to give you a road map to follow. In this way, you are less likely to veer off your chosen path.

Every journey starts with a first step. To avoid being overwhelmed, think baby steps, not grand leaps. Choose one thing to improve incrementally every day, like replacing industrial orange juice drinks with a handful of fresh oranges to meet your goal of eating healthier. Eating fruit like an apple or a banana is something most of us can commit to, instead of consuming fizzy drinks and pastries. With every success, you gain the confidence and motivation to take a bigger leap. Small successes build upon one another to create momentum. In other words, goal setting is an ongoing process, not just a means to an end. Be prepared for a long but satisfying journey.

VISUALIZE

Close your eyes. Imagine biting into a lemon. Did you salivate? There's a good chance that you did. Visualization has a powerful effect on the mind.

The images that we create in our minds affect our thoughts and actions. This is why virtually all top performers in every profession, from athletes to surgeons, actors to musicians and business executives, will perform the action in their mind before doing it in reality to improve their performance.

Basketball legend Michael Jordan always pictured the last shot in his mind before he threw a hoop.

Boxing legend Muhammad Ali pictured himself victorious long before the actual boxing match.

"Imagination's everything. It is the preview of life's coming attractions."

~*Albert Einstein*

Take time to use the power of your creative mind to conjure vivid images of your goal. If you wish to create a new hair shampoo, picture how lustrous and shiny your hair will look. If you wish to create a modelling agency for children, imagine smart confident little boys and girls with broad smiles.

CREATE A SCHEDULE

Once you have identified and prioritised your goals, set up a schedule to get the work done. Start each morning by devising your "priorities list." What are the top three projects that have to get done for the day? Where can you shine? Itemize them and start these most important tasks first. Let everything else revolve around your plan and not the other way around. Analyse your schedule, your responsibilities and daily tasks, and figure out what you must do immediately and what can wait. If you want to have meaningful days, you've got to be committed to making the day meaningful. Creating a prioritized list will help you focus, be more reliable and conquer work overload. It will also reduce stress because you won't have to be worried that you've neglected to do something important. And in addition you'll be more productive because your time and energy will focus on high-value activities.

Four Questions to reflect on:

- What are your top `THREE goals in life?

- What resources will you need to achieve your goals?"

- What could potentially stop you from achieving these goals?

- Knowing all you know above, what is the first step you will take going forward in life?

Now it's time to write a farewell message to your old self. After reading this book and ready to **SHIFT**, what would you say to your old self:

Dear Self,

Your new self,

_____

(insert your name and date)

CONCLUSION

The difference between the woman who wakes up and acts upon her dream and another who sits around making excuses is the following: the former lives a fulfilling life and leaves behind a legacy while the latter just passes through. We all have a purpose. We all are called but very few recognize this opportunity. Take your best shot at the life you've been given. Be positively contagious and help others do the same.

On your way to becoming a highly confident and successful woman, you will inevitably come across forks in the road, stop signs, and rocks. View every obstacle as an opportunity or a learning experience and keep marching on. Don't let the noise around you overshadow your dream. Filter the noise. It's just noise. Accessorise with your Confidence Pearls wherever you go. The world is waiting for your rising!

"We all go through rainy days. Whether we choose to dance in the rain or just stay soaked is a mindset. It's not about the presence of the rain. It's the hope and promising future of a rainbow after the rain."

~Mofoluwaso Ilevbare

PERSONAL REFLECTION

Imagine you are 99 years old and sitting in your favourite rocking chair reminiscing how your life unfolded in the following areas; Spiritual, Emotional, Physical, Mental & Social, what you did for Fun and Leisure, lessons you learnt, people you met, and your leadership or service in the community. Now take your pen and jot down:

- How do you truly feel?

- What are you most proud of?

- What is your evidence that you lived a meaningful life?

- What three words do people use to describe you ?

- Are these words being used to describe you TODAY?

- If YES, what can you do to further strengthen these words?

- If NO, what needs to shift in your life to make you who you really desire to be?

HELLO!

This ends our journey together but it is also a beginning for better things to come.

What was most helpful for you? Please tell me. I'd love to hear from you. Simply send an email to info@mofoluwasoilevbare.com. I respond promptly to every message and look forward to seeing yours soon. If this book inspired you, you can also leave a review on Amazon to encourage someone else to purchase a copy or spread the message by purchasing a copy as a gift for someone.

ABOUT THE AUTHOR

Mofoluwaso Ilevbare is a Confidence & Peak Performance Coach empowering women everywhere to take the lid off, to Dare. Dream. and Deliver, to truly be unstoppable at work and life.

Mofoluwaso is also a testament of God's faithfulness. She has been to death's doorway and back, not once, but twice in her life! After narrowly escaping the onslaught of death via flying bullets, she has purposed in her heart to make an indelible mark in this world. This commitment has inspired her to see everyday as an awesome opportunity to help others get rid of fear, stress, and anxiety so they can be truly authentic and enjoy great success.

Mofoluwaso has a Bachelor in Pharmacy, a Master's in Business Administration and coaching certifications in Social and Emotional Intelligence, Conversational Intelligence. She is also a member of the John Maxwell Team, a 4-time Amazon Bestselling author and has developed several other heart-centred resources such as The Confidence Journal For Career Women, Uplift Your Productivity, and the Love Cafe devotional series.

As an advocate for women empowerment, Mofoluwaso lives this passion as a Cherie Blair Foundation Women Mentor and Founder of two non-profit organizations improving communities in Oyo State, Nigeria.

A soulful thought leader, wife, and mother of two boys. Mofoluwaso is proud to profess she loves God, family, life coaching—and also has a healthy appetite for chocolate cake. She maintains an active blog at www.mofoluwasoilevbare.com and has been featured in Huffington Post, Executive Women, Channels TV, and many more.

Visit https://mofoluwasoilevbare.com/ to learn more about Mofoluwaso and the inspiring work she does with her clients each day. For a free 30mins strategy session, you can find her calendar here http://bit.ly/calendarbooking. You can also connect with her on Facebook , Twitter, Instagram and LinkedIn.

REFERENCES

1. Retrieved from http://www.independent.co.uk/arts-entertainment/tv/features/meet-africas-oprah-why-mosunmola-mo-abudu wants-to-change-the-worlds-view-of-her-continent-8940635.html

2. Gundan, F. (2013). The 20 Young Power Women In Africa 2013. Retrieved from http://www.forbes.com/sites/mfonobongnsehe/2013/12/04/the-20-young-power-women-in-africa-2013/#3988c0b87231

3-4. Singh, R. (2012). Women entrepreneurship issues, challenges and empowerment through self help groups: an overview of Himachal Pradesh. International Journal of Democratic and Development Studies, 1(1), 45–58.

5. Retrieved from http://www.biznisafrica.co.za/engen-mauritius-md-named-one-of-africas-most-influential-women-in-chemical-sector/

6. Gundan, F. (2013). The 20 Young Power Women In Africa 2013. Retrieved from http://www.forbes.com/sites/mfonobongnsehe/2013/12/04/the-20-young-power-women-in-africa 2013/#3988c0b87231

7. Retrieved from http:// www.premaeskincare.com

8. Retrieved from
http://www.thealishanicole.com/blog/2015/2/9/herstory
-with-erica-nicole-of-yfs-magazine

9. Retrieved from http://www.cvent.com/events/black-
enterprise-women-of-power-summit/faqs-
dd9133b9194647a78183ed84670ce1cf.aspx

10. Retrieved from
https://www.blackentrepreneurprofile.com/profile-
full/article/adenike-ogunlesi/

11. Retrieved from
http://www.fastcompany.com/3009143/most-creative-
people-2013/62-bethlehem-tilahun-alemu

OTHER BOOKS BY THE AUTHOR

THE CONFIDENCE
JOURNAL FOR CAREER
WOMEN

Copyright © 2016

UPLIFT YOUR
PRODUCTIVITY

9 Strategies To Maximize Your Time
& Optimize Your Life

Copyright © 2016

THE LOVE CAFE
DEVOTIONAL - FOR
COUPLES

Copyright © 2015

Books are available on amazon

Made in the USA
Charleston, SC
10 March 2017